| F | U | TH | O | R | K |

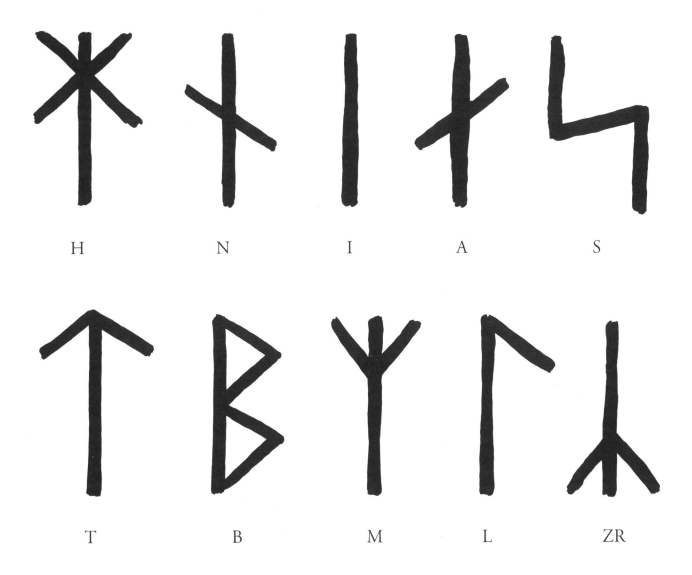

| H | N | I | A | S |

| T | B | M | L | ZR |

You will need these Viking rune shapes for the projects on pages 4, 8 and 22. See opposite for how to use them.

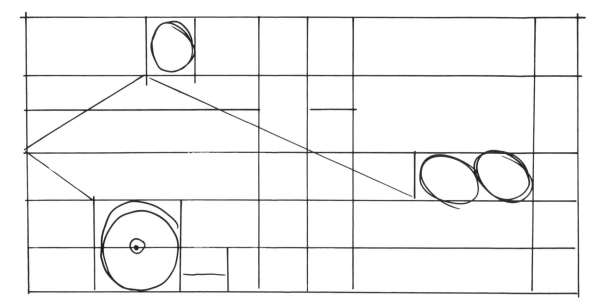

Draw the goddess Freya. Were her cats called Kevin and Keith?

CONTENTS

Whatever you choose to make first you'll need plenty of packaging, so it's a good idea to start collecting it in advance. Ask people to save things for you instead of throwing them away.

You can flatten cardboard boxes and cereal packets to save space. Rinse plastic bottles and leave them to dry. Prepare an area to work in and have lots of old newspapers handy if you are using glue and paints.

Calm down Birni, it's just a bit of fun!

Berserkers are OK, so long as you don't upset them.

1

HOW TO MAKE A HELMET

For a Viking in battle against axes and swords, his helmet was his best friend. The basic model came in metal or leather. Added extras included a spike on top, a neck guard and a nose protector. Unfortunately, those fantastic helmets with horns probably never existed on the battlefield.

YOU'LL NEED:
Card: 1 strip 64 x 3 cm and 2 strips 38 x 3 cm, bubble plastic (with small bubbles) 50 x 20 cm, glue, scissors, marker pen, acrylic metallic paints and brush.

HARALD THE HOUSE HUSBAND?

See page 16.

1 Fit the long card strip around your head. Glue the ends together.

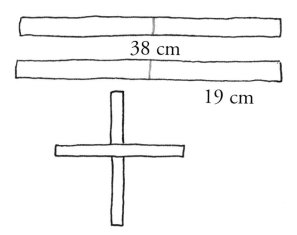

38 cm

19 cm

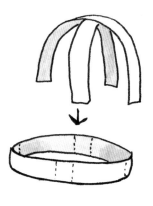

2 Mark the centres of the other two strips and glue together to form a cross.

3 Position the ends equally inside the headband. Mark and glue.

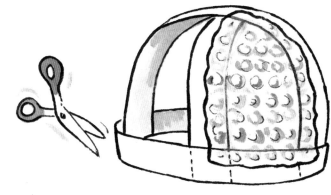

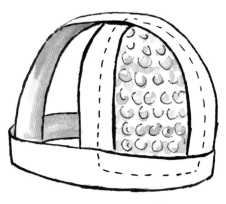

4 Mark and cut out four pieces of bubble plastic 1.5 cm bigger than the spaces between the strips.

5 Glue to the inside of the card strips.

TOP TIP – TOP TIP
You can use shorter strips of card from cereal boxes by sticking two together.

6 Paint to look like metal. Use thick blobs of acrylic paint to look like rivets.

How To Make A Shield

A Falkyr (or Valkyr) was a Norse war goddess. They flew to earth on their winged horses collecting the dead warriors from the battlefield to live forever with the gods in Valhalla. The Vikings believed the Aurora Borealis was the light glinting off the Valkyries' shields.

TOP TIP – TOP TIP
Look for pictures of Viking shields to see the different designs painted on them.

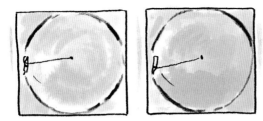

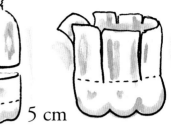

Fold back.

5 cm

1 Use the pencil tied to the nail to draw a circle 50 cm in diameter on the cardboard squares. Cut them out.

2 Cut the bottle in half. Make six equal cuts to the bottom half as shown.

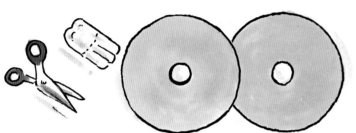

Front   Back

3 Cut bottle-sized holes in the centres of the cardboard circles.

4 Push the bottom of the bottle through one of the holes. Bend over the cut plastic and glue to the cardboard.

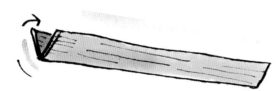

5 Fold and glue the strip of cardboard in half lengthways.

6 Place across the hole and glue.

7 Glue the two circles of cardboard together. Make sure the corrugations go in opposite ways for maximum strength.

8 Finish off with acrylic paint. Write your name on it with runes (see page 22).

HOW TO MAKE A MAILSHIRT

The sagas told of the most important Vikings going into battle wearing a byrnie. This was a protective shirt made of interlocking iron rings. Of course, spears and arrows could poke through the holes, so they wore padding underneath - the more the better!

BULKY BYRNIE
A typical sized mailshirt had 30,000 rings and weighed 12 kilogrammes.

← 100 cm →

1 Fold the bubble plastic in half.

2 Lay the T-shirt on top. Draw round it with the marker pen.

3 Carefully cut out the shape and a slot for your head.

4 Tape both sides together as shown.

5 Turn inside out.

6 Paint to look like metal with grey and silver acrylic paint. Wear a belt or weave one (see page 16).

TOP TIP – TOP TIP
Make a berserker bearskin cloak with a piece of brown fun fur. Use a button badge painted gold as a clasp.

BERSERKERS WERE FEARLESS WARRIORS WHO WORKED THEMSELVES INTO A FRENZY. VERY SCARY!

HOW TO MAKE A WARRIOR'S AXE

Vikings were the first to use the two-handed axe. It certainly scared their enemies and did its job well. The only problem was that while swinging the axe over their heads, their shields got in the way and had to be slung over their back, leaving them an easy target for keen-eyed archers or spearsmen. Ouch!

YOU'LL NEED:
Corrugated cardboard 25 x 50 cm (with corrugations lengthways), card (cereal box) 32 x 15 cm, pencil, masking tape, tracing paper, scissors, ruler, acrylic paints and brushes, stencils, PVA glue.

TOP TIP - TOP TIP
Don't cut through the top fold of the axe head!

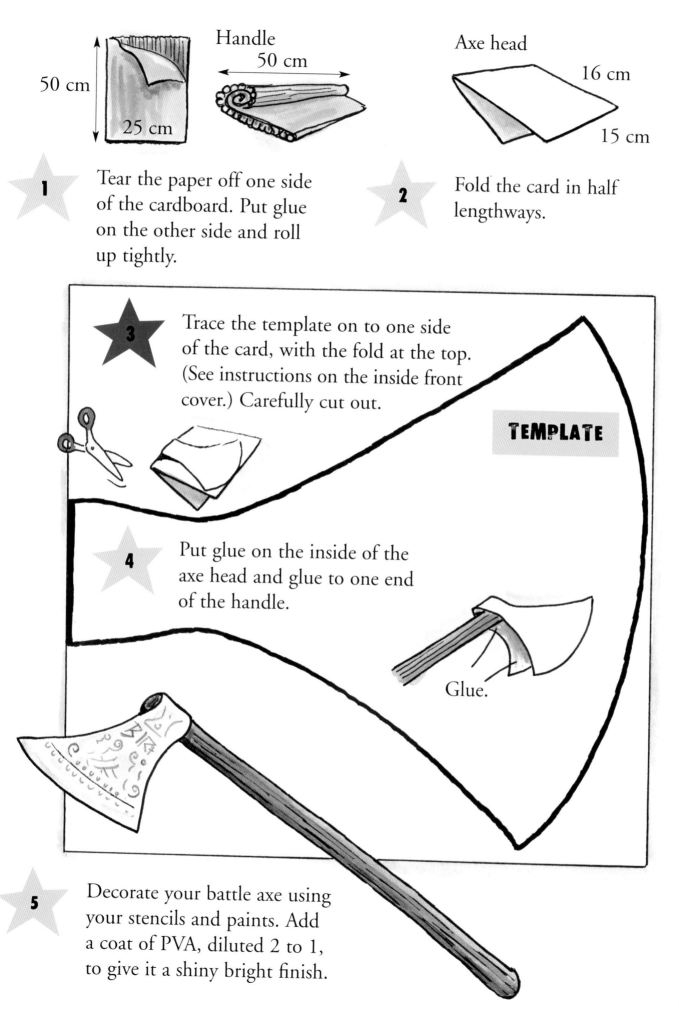

Handle
50 cm

Axe head
16 cm
15 cm

50 cm
25 cm

1 Tear the paper off one side of the cardboard. Put glue on the other side and roll up tightly.

2 Fold the card in half lengthways.

3 Trace the template on to one side of the card, with the fold at the top. (See instructions on the inside front cover.) Carefully cut out.

TEMPLATE

4 Put glue on the inside of the axe head and glue to one end of the handle.

Glue.

5 Decorate your battle axe using your stencils and paints. Add a coat of PVA, diluted 2 to 1, to give it a shiny bright finish.

HOW TO DISCOVER AMERICA

The Icelandic Sagas tell the story of Eric the Red, his son, Leif the Lucky, and how they discovered Greenland and America.

YOU'LL NEED:
To discover Greenland first, a nice sturdy longboat, plenty of warriors, some berserkers to frighten the natives, 6 months' supply of dried fish and the luck of the gods.

GREENLAND?
Eric the Red sailed from Iceland to Greenland in AD 982. He called it Greenland to persuade other people to settle there.

The only thing green here is Siggi the Seasick.

VINLAND
About 20 years later, Eric's son, Leif, sailed further west and discovered America. He called it Vinland.

When you see the second polar bear, turn left.

SNORRI BABY

The sagas tell of a baby being born in Vinland. They called him Snorri.

SKRAELINGS

But fierce fighting with the Skraelings who lived there already, forced the settlers to return to Greenland.

PROOF

In 1960 the remains of a Viking camp were found at L'Anse aux Meadows in Canada. Carbon dating said it was about 1000 years old.

DID VIKINGS STAY IN AMERICA?

Some people think they became part of Native American tribes like the Mandan.

11

VIKING VOYAGES

Vikings were the best sailors and shipbuilders around. They raided and traded across Europe and the North Atlantic for over 300 years.

EDGE OF THE WORLD

Settlers struggled to live on the icy edge of Greenland for nearly 400 years, then vanished. It could have been because of climate change, disease or fighting with the Skraelings. What do you think happened?

GREENLAND

THAT WAS LUCKY

They settled in Iceland and sailed west to discover Greenland. From there, Leif the Lucky sailed further west and landed in America.

MARKLAND (LABRADOR)

L'ANSE AUX MEADOWS

NEWFOUNDLAND

VINLAND

VIKING RAIDERS

They raided the coasts of the British Isles and France. They set up their own kingdoms in Eastern England, Ireland, the Scottish Islands and Normandy (land of the Northmen).

MAP KEY
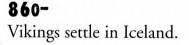
➡ Viking voyages
● Viking territory

790-800
Vikings begin raiding the British Isles.

860-
Vikings settle in Iceland.

960-
Harald Bluetooth, King of Denmark and Norway, becomes a Christian.

LONG SHIPS   SHORT TEMPERS

RUS Я US

Vikings from Sweden sailed up and down the great rivers of Eastern Europe and founded the first Russian state called Rus.

ICELAND

FAROES

NORWAY

SWEDEN

SHETLAND ISLANDS

NOVGOROD

SCOTLAND

RIVER DWINA

RIVER VOLGA

DUBLIN

YORK

RUS

IRELAND

KIEV

RIVER DNIEPER

HEDEBY

DENMARK

DANELAW

ANGLO-SAXON ENGLAND

NORMANDY

BYZANTIUM

SICILY

1000
Leif Eriksson lands in America.

1066
Harald Hardrada, King of Norway, killed near York. The last Viking invasion of England.

1190–1320
Icelandic Sagas written down.

HOW TO MAKE A VIKING PANCAKE

As well as defending their village while the men were away, Viking women did all the cooking. It was their responsibility to store enough spare food, after harvest or a hunting expedition, to feed their families perhaps for a whole year. Try this pancake and compare it to a modern one. The Vikings used any fruit or berries that were in season.

KITCHENWARE YOU'LL NEED:
Mixing bowl, whisk, dessertspoon, teaspoon, sharp knife, chopping board, non-stick frying-pan, spatula.

INGREDIENTS YOU'LL NEED:
35 g white flour, 30 g wholemeal flour, ¼ teaspoon salt, 175 ml milk, small eating apple, ½ teaspoon butter for each pancake, runny honey to drizzle over. **Makes 5 pancakes of about 11 cm diameter.**

TOP TIP - TOP TIP
Cook one at a time until you get the hang of it.

14

 First, wash your hands.

 Wash, core and chop the apple as small as you can.

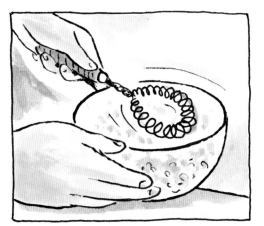

3 Mix all the ingredients except the butter and honey together gently.

4 Get an adult to help with this step. Melt butter in the frying-pan and when it sizzles pour in 3 dessertspoons of batter.

 Cook with a steady sizzle for about 2 minutes each side. Turn it using the spatula.

 Serve with a drizzle of honey. Take care – they are very hot.

HOW TO MAKE A LUCET

The Vikings found a brilliant way to make a single strand of wire or string much stronger. They wound it round a lucet which wove it together to make a long decorative cord. It was an early form of knitting. Done with soft string, the cords could be made into bracelets or drawstrings for bags and purses.

YOU'LL NEED:
Plastic fork, ball of wool, cord or string, sticky tack.

Knut the Knotty wants extra forks and I'm not arguing!

BURGERVIKING

1 Snap the middle prong off the fork to leave only the two end ones.

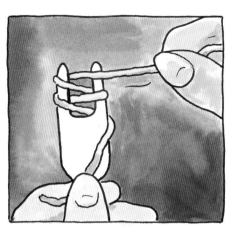

★ **2** With the fork facing you, wind wool on as shown.

★ **3** Wind it behind the right prong, in front of the left, through to the front and hold out as shown.

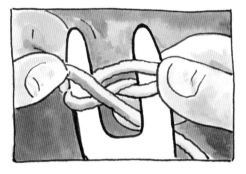

★ **4** Push the stitches down with your thumb. Wiggle the lower stitch over the top one and off the prong. Pull the loose end slightly to tighten stitches.

★ **5** Hold the thread out and turn the fork towards you so the back is facing you as in the picture. Wiggle lower stitch over top one again.

★ **6** Keep turning fork round and wiggling bottom stitch over until the chain is long enough. To cast off, cut the wool from the ball, thread through loops and pull it tight.

TOP TIP - TOP TIP
Stick a blob of sticky tack on the fork when you stop so the stitches don't fall off.

GOD DAYS

In English, the names of six days of the week come directly from the old Norse and old English. (The old English is in brackets here.) They replaced the names of the Roman gods, which the days had been named after. Saturday, or Saturn's day, is the odd one out. For a Viking, Saturday was bath day!

 SUNDAY
SOL (SUNNE)

 MONDAY
MANI

Sol, the sun is a girl. Mani, the moon is a boy. They drive their chariots across the sky chased by a pack of savage wolves. If they are caught, the world will end.

 TUESDAY
TYR (TIW)

Tyr, the one-handed god of war. Bitten off by the wolf giant, Fenris, who'd love to get hold of the other one.

 WEDNESDAY
ODIN (WODEN)

Odin, riding on his eight-legged horse, Sleipnir, made the world and placed the sun and moon in the sky.

 THURSDAY
THOR

Red-haired son of Odin, makes the thunder and lightning by striking his hammer.

FRIDAY
FREYA and FRIGG

Frigg is the wife of Odin and mother of the Earth. Freya, goddess of love and queen of the elves, rides in a chariot drawn by two giant cats.

 SATURDAY
LAUGAR

Laugar is the old Norse word for 'bath'. Not only bath day, it also belonged to Loki, the god of mischief!

I'm taking my axe, just in case.

SVEN THE SUSPICIOUS MY SAUNA

18

HOW TO PLAN A VIKING WEEK

Sail through the week with this weekly planner. You can write the date and month on if you like. Each A4 piece of paper will last for two weeks. Then you can replace it with a fresh one.

YOU'LL NEED:
Card 430 x 280 cm, pencil, ruler, masking tape, tracing paper, A4 paper, scissors, craft knife, felt-tip pens, paints and brushes, sticky tack.

4 cm x 7

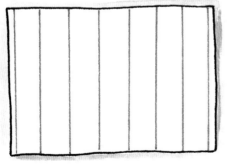

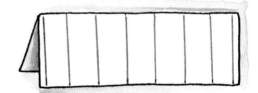

 1   Draw lines to divide the A4 paper into seven columns, each 4 cm wide, leaving a small margin.

2   Fold in half lengthways.

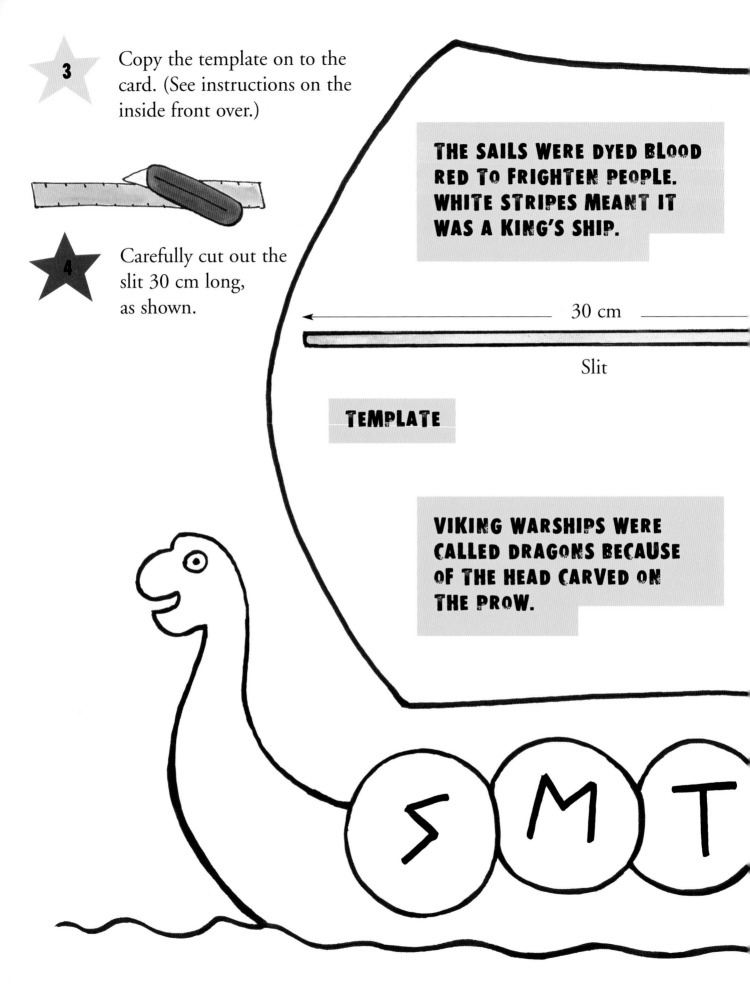

3 Copy the template on to the card. (See instructions on the inside front over.)

4 Carefully cut out the slit 30 cm long, as shown.

THE SAILS WERE DYED BLOOD RED TO FRIGHTEN PEOPLE. WHITE STRIPES MEANT IT WAS A KING'S SHIP.

30 cm

Slit

TEMPLATE

VIKING WARSHIPS WERE CALLED DRAGONS BECAUSE OF THE HEAD CARVED ON THE PROW.

⭐ 5   Use your paints and pens to decorate the ship. Add seven stripes to the sail and draw in a Viking crew.

⭐ 6   Slot the A4 paper through the slit and use as a daily notepad. Change the paper round every week. Stick to the wall with sticky tack.

HOW TO WRITE RUNES

The knowledge of the runes was passed to mankind by the Norse Gods. 'Rune' means 'secret' and each one has a magical meaning as well as being a letter of the alphabet. They are made of straight lines so they could easily be carved into wood or stone.

YOUR STENCIL SHEET

There were many versions of the runes, but this is one used by the Vikings from about AD 700-1100. It is called FUTHORK after the sounds made by the first six symbols.

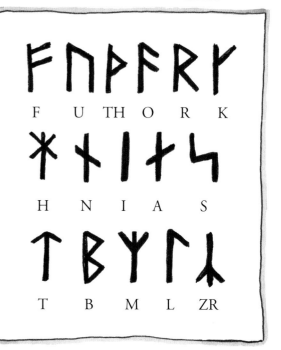

Use this chart to write your name and secret magic spells in runes. There are only 16 symbols, so some are used again for similar sounds.

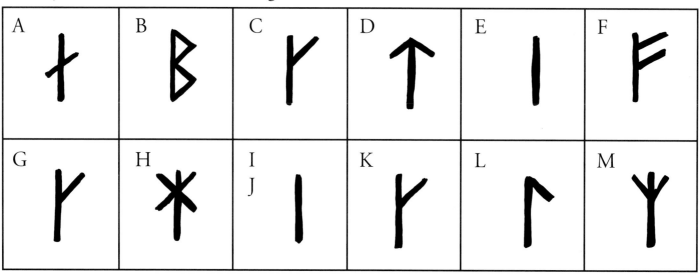

Draw a long fierce snake to write your runes in.
The Vikings used a dot to separate words.

ALL VIKINGS HAD NICKNAMES, HARALD BLUETOOTH, KING OF NORWAY, LOVED EATING BLUEBERRIES.

RUNE STONES
Large stones were carved to mark special events.

RUNE MAGIC
Runes were carved on small pieces of wood and used to tell the future.

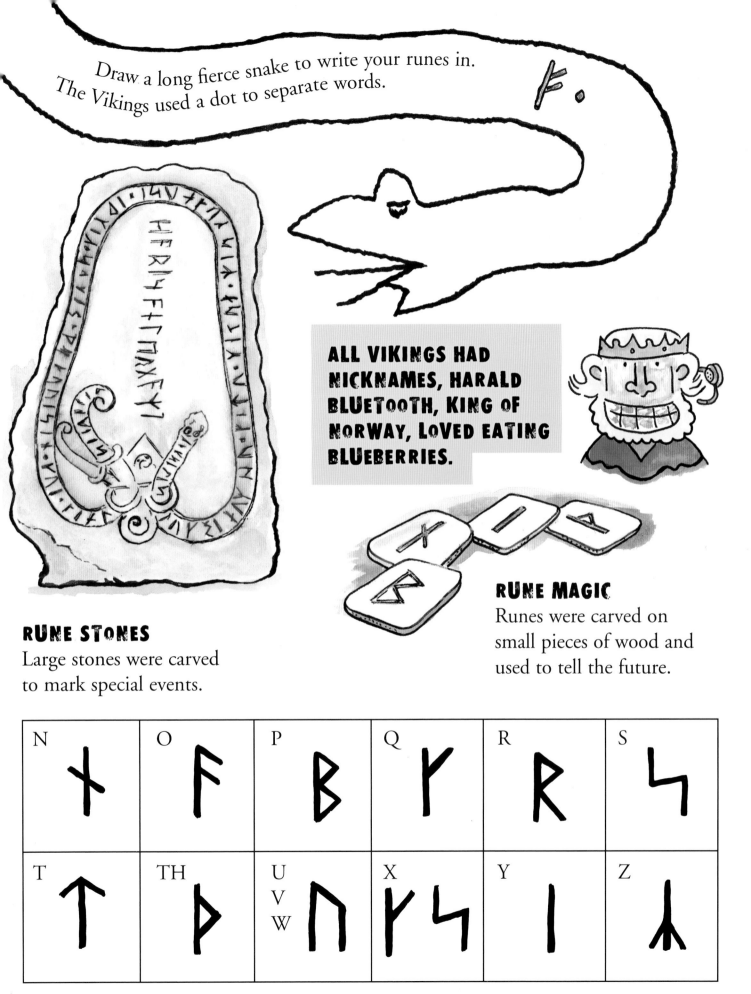

N	O	P	Q	R	S
↑	F	B	Y	R	Ϟ

T	TH	U V W	X	Y	Z
↑	Þ	ᚢ	ᚷ	I	ᛉ

HOW TO USE YOUR STENCILS

If you have the stencil edition, cut or tear the stencil sheet from the back of the book. Choose a rune, place it over your paper and secure with masking tape. Holding a pencil, crayon or pen in an upright position, shade in the inside of the stencil. If you do this with a thin pen or pencil, it should look like it has been scratched out of wood or stone. If you have the hardback edition, copy or draw the runes yourself using the instructions at the front of the book.

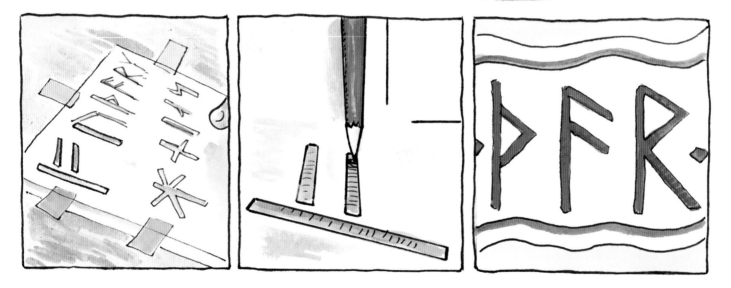

TOP TIP – TOP TIP
Get an ancient wood or stone effect by putting different textured surfaces under your paper.

1

Place the paper on top of your stencil and rub over it with a pencil or crayon. This will give the rune a carved-out look.

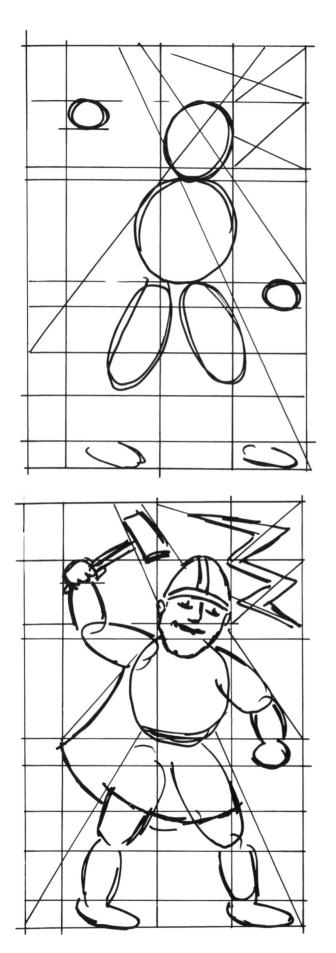

Draw the great god Thor with his mighty hammer.

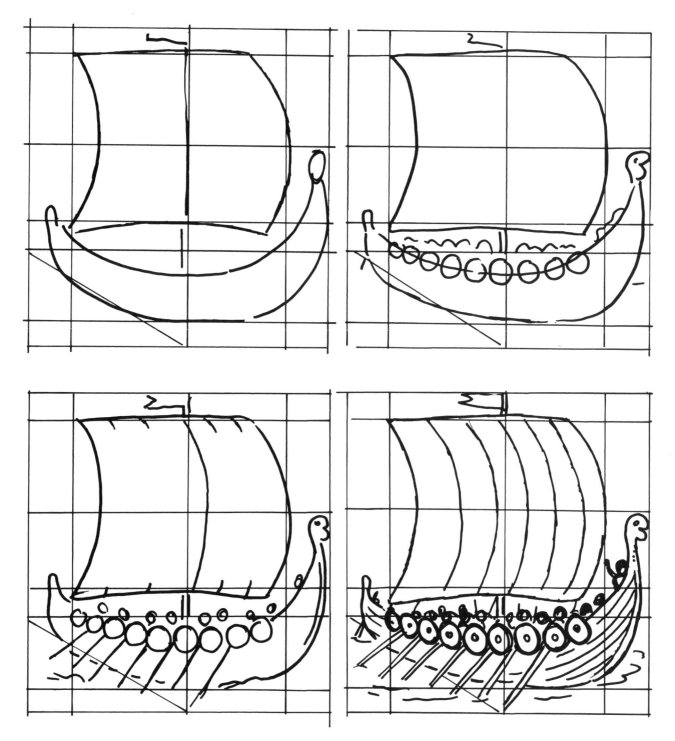

Draw a Viking longship.